ISBN 10: 1475224230

ISBN 13: 9781475224238

1

**Top Tips:** Interviewing

2

# INSTITUTE OF DIRECTORS

**"Top Tips: Interviewing** is a quick and easy pragmatic guide which gets straight to the point, making it a valuable resource for interviewers and interviewees alike!"

**Ryan Ahern**
*Director of Learning and Development*
*Institute of Directors*

# Top Tips:
# Interviewing

## by John Hodgson

4

# CONTENTS

# INTRODUCTION

The **Top Tips** series of mini books is a compendium of short, 20-30 minute reads.

Forty years of experience condensed into a series of 10 mini books. Each one takes less than 30 minutes to read and each one is a '*masterpiece of condensed learning*'.

A must for busy individuals who don't have the time to attend a training course on all 10 subjects covered in this unique series.

The first book to be published in the series is ***Top Tips: Interviewing***. It has been written, primarily, with the INTERVIEWEE in mind. However, during research, it became clear that fewer than 10% of interviewers had received training in interviewing skills and techniques. *Chapter 4* is directed towards INTERVIEWERS.

As we enter 2012, '*business failures*', '*business down-sizing*' and '*redundancies*' have become all too familiar headlines. One widely forecast effect of these is an increase in unemployment. The knock-on effect of which is **more** people chasing **fewer** jobs. A recent survey suggests that for every job vacancy there may be as many as 40 applicants and, in extreme cases, 200-300.

Fewer jobs. More applicants. Never before has the need to prepare for an interview been more important.

# Who Should Read This Book?

If you have expectations of being interviewed in the near future and would like to improve your chances of being offered the job, you will most certainly benefit from reading this book.

If you are soon to graduate from school, college or university and have little or no experience of job interviews then this book will give you a strong idea of what to expect and how to deal with it.

Maybe you have already attended interviews and wonder why you've not been offered a job. If so, you may find the answer here. Investing 30 minutes of your time to read this book could turn out to be the best investment you make this year.

If you are planning to interview somebody in the near future, but have not yet received formal training, you too will benefit from reading this book.

Apart from interviewees and interviewers, any parent or grandparent who wants to help their children or grandchildren make a success of their lives.

More often than not, your son or daughter will be more willing to listen to an outsider with a proven track record than to a family member – even if that family member has a successful background.

## CV (Curriculum Vitae) aka Résumé

To avoid confusion, this book contains **Top Tips** on the interview alone. It does not contain tips on writing a CV or Résumé. These can be found in a separate 30 minute mini book.

# TOP TIPS: PREPARATION

## Let's get started...

Preparation means doing your homework. Find out as much as you can about the company, industry and competition. One of the best sources will be the **company website**.

✓ Look for the company's *Mission Statement* and *Vision Statement*, should they have one.

One, often overlooked, source of information is the company's *Annual Report and Accounts*. If the company is listed on the stock exchange, this information will be in the public domain and simple to attain. Call the company secretary's office or go online and download a copy. Your aim should be to get a hard copy: it will be in colour and **demonstrate your effort to learn about the company**.

In the UK, all limited liability companies will have Ltd or Limited after their name and they must, by law, file their annual accounts at **Companies House**. For a modest sum, you will be able to download the company accounts to your computer.

The Annual Report and Accounts will, typically, begin with a statement from the company Chairman or CEO and contain a *Profit and Loss Account* or *Balance Sheet*. Don't be intimidated if you don't know how to read the accounts, the opening statement will tell you all that you need to know about **where the company has come from** (last year's lows and highs) and its **vision of the future**. This will be followed with reports from senior operating officers.

In case you're wondering what you'd find in a *Profit & Loss Account* or *Balance Sheet* here's the briefest of summaries. A *P&L* shows the value of sales, associated costs and the net profit. A *Balance Sheet* is a 'financial snapshot' that shows what the company owes and owns at a frozen moment in time.

You may be the ONLY candidate to turn up to the interview with a copy of the latest set of accounts. If not the only one, you will certainly be one of the few.

✓ Every industry has a **trade magazine** or **trade newspaper**. Find out what it is and get the latest edition.

You can be sure that the person interviewing you will be familiar with the main stories and articles. Don't try to show how smart you are by quoting from it – that could backfire on you. Instead, use it to **build your knowledge of industry trends**.

> eg.
> The publishing industry is currently going through a massive change. There are now estimated to be over 6 million Kindle owners. E-books have arrived, bringing with them a new generation of previously unknown authors. Many books are free. Others can be purchased online for £0.99 or $0.99 depending on where you are located.
> Kindle users have also found a new way of using the device: it's simple to download files and documents and to have huge amounts of information at their fingertips during meetings.
> If your interview was with Amazon, you would do well to know about these issues.

During your own upcoming interview you may well be tested to see if you have any understanding or knowledge of any **changes affecting the industry** that may soon become *your* industry.

✓ Find out about the recruiting company which has been hired to do the interviewing. Read their publications and current areas of investigation.

Consider the newspaper carrying the advertisement. From this you can deduce the readership and the cost. An ad in a national publication will cost more and be **aimed to reach more people** than a small ad in a local newspaper. It may indicate that the company is **willing to contribute to relocation costs**.

✓ Be sure you know the **exact location** of the interview.

You may arrive in good time only to face an unexpected choice of buildings, floors etc. If possible, make a trial run and time the journey.

✓ Arrive a few minutes **early**.

✓ Take extra copies of your CV **and** a copy of the advertisement if there was one.

✓ Don't forget to take copies of **references** and **testimonials** with you.

Check the date/s to make sure they're all **current** – a 10 year old reference might make *you* happy but it's not relevant today. It could actually work against you.

✓ Check your **appearance**. Think carefully about the role you're applying for and wear something appropriate. **You only get one chance to make a first impression.**

It has been said that some interviewers make up their mind about the suitability of a candidate within **10 seconds** of seeing them walk into a room. Your **body language** will send out a message in an instant.

✓ Stand tall, walk with purpose, smile and wait to be invited to take a seat.

10

There are, of course, jobs where it's deemed essential to make a favourable and instant impression.

   ✓  **Be prepared**.

# KPIs

In December 2011 I was invited by Anglia Ruskin University to deliver a master class to students at the Lord Ashcroft International Business Centre in Cambridge. The audience consisted of students about to leave formal education to embark on their respective careers.

At one point I used the acronym 'KPI' and received blank looks. It means **Key Performance Indicator** and is a term used by every organisation to define how the company measures its performance. However, not one of my master class students had heard of the phrase and I was reminded of a lesson learned in my own youth. **Never assume**.

Since every organisation uses KPIs, it makes sense for you to give some thought to the type of performance measurements that the company you are hoping to join is likely to use.

### Examples of different KPIs

A retailer might use '*sales per square foot*' as a Key Performance Indicator. Other commonly used KPIs in retailing are: '*sales per week*', '*sales by product*', '*sales by department*' and '*sales by location*'.

Hotels use a unique KPI described as '*occupancy*'. This is the comparison between the number of rooms available and the number occupied; it is usually expressed as a percentage. Empty rooms, just like empty seats on an aircraft, are lost opportunity costs.

On the other hand, magazine publishers will most certainly be interested in '*monthly advertising revenue*'. ' *Industry average*' is another widely used benchmark. In consumer products, '*market share*' or '*brand share*' are commonly used as indicators.

Simply put, **different industries use different KPIs.** When asked if you have any questions, **this is a good question to ask**.

I have yet to come across any organisation not interested in increasing sales and profit. These are universal KPIs.

# Before entering the interview room.

- ✓ **Switch off** your mobile/cell phone.

- ✓ Check that you have a **pen** to make notes. Chances are, you won't be expected to write, but just imagine the impression you'll create if you have to ask to borrow a pen! Not good.

- ✓ Check your **appearance**: hair, nails, shoes, buttons and zip!

- ✓ **Plan ahead** and consider what you might reasonably be expected to produce on the day. Searching through your briefcase and not finding it immediately may convey the impression that you are disorganised. Make sure you know where everything is.

- ✓ Create your own **pre-flight checklist**: every pilot has one regardless of the number of hours flown.

If, during your pre-flight routine, you see papers and files in your briefcase that will not be required, remove them. Should you need to retrieve a document from your briefcase during the interview you need to be able to locate it quickly, without fumbling. Your aim must be to come across as **efficient** and **well-organised.**

# When interviewed by a panel.

You may face more than one interviewer.

[Image courtesy of: Carter Green's Business Centre in West Bromwich, Midlands. Rooms available to hire at www.cartersgeeensbusinesscentre.co.uk]

✗ Don't fall into the trap of addressing the most senior person all the time. He or she might be called out of the meeting and then you'll be left with people you've ignored.

✓ **Be alert**. Panelists sometimes have hidden agendas. One might be looking to hire someone with specific experience, whilst another might be looking for somebody with the right mental attitude and willingness to challenge conventional thinking.

✗ Don't ignore the secretary or assistant. In life there are decision makers and people of influence. Secretaries and assistants are most definitely in the second category.

# What can you do if the interviewer is untrained?

There is a possibility that the interviewer may not have had formal training. Don't worry! If you've done your homework, your preparation will show and be favourably received.

You will not face an untrained interviewer if you are being screened by a recruitment consultant. They will most certainly bring structure to the meeting and a list of pre-prepared questions.

*See Chapter 3: 'Top 50 Interview Questions with Answers'.*

# Fail to prepare and prepare to fail.

Interviewers expect a candidate to be able to review their work history in detail. Be prepared to tell the interviewer the names of the companies you have worked for, your job title, your starting and ending dates of employment, how much you earned and what the job entailed.

You would be surprised at how many job applicants cannot remember what they put in their job application. Don't be one of them!

✓ Before the interview **refresh** your memory. Take another look at your CV. Consider the questions that may arise so you can speak about your work history with **confidence**, in **detail** and with **accuracy**.

# TOP 50 INTERVIEW QUESTIONS

1.  Tell me about yourself.

2.  What do you know about our company?

3.  What experience do you have in this field?

4.  Do you consider yourself successful?

5.  How would your work colleagues describe you?

6.  Why did you leave your last job?

7.  What have you done to improve your knowledge in the last year?

8.  Are you applying for other jobs?

9.  Why do you want to work for this organisation?

10. Do you know anyone who works for us?

11. What kind of salary are you looking for?

12. Are you a team player?

13. How long would you expect to work for us if hired?

14. Have you ever had to fire anyone? How did you feel about it?

15. What is your philosophy toward work?

16. What are your goals for the future? Or... Where do you see yourself in five years?

17. Have you ever been asked to leave a position?

18. Explain how you would be an asset to this organisation.

19. Why should we hire you?

20. Tell me about a time when you worked in a successful team and what made it successful.

21. What irritates you most about your co-workers?

22. What is your greatest strength?

23. Do you have a weakness?

24. Why do you think you would do well at this job?

25. Tell me about your plans for *Continuing Personal Development.*

26. What kind of person would you refuse to work with?

27. What is more important to you: the money or the work?

28. What would your previous supervisor say is your strongest point?

29. Tell me about a problem you have had with a supervisor.

30. What has disappointed you about a job?

31. Tell me about your ability to work under pressure.

32. Who else have you applied to or have interviews with?

33. What motivates you to do your best on the job?

34. What lessons have you learned from your previous bosses?

35. How would you know you were successful in this job?

36. Would you be willing to relocate if the job required it?

37. What have you learned from your mistakes?

38. **Give me an example of something you accomplished and something you were disappointed with.**

39. **What have you learned from mistakes on the job?**

40. **Do you have any** *blind spots*?

41. **If you were hiring a person for this job, what would you look for?**

42. **How would you describe customer service?**

43. **How do you propose to compensate for your lack of experience?**

44. **What qualities do you look for in a boss?**

45. **Tell me about a time when you helped resolve a dispute between others.**

46. **What position do you prefer in a team working on a project?**

47. **Who inspires you and why?**

48. **What has been your biggest professional disappointment?**

49. **Tell me about the most fun you have had on a job.**

50. **Do you have any questions for me?**

You may like to take a few minutes to think about how *you* would answer these questions before moving on to the suggested answers.

# TOP 50 INTERVIEW QUESTIONS WITH SUGGESTED ANSWERS

Listed below are the most common questions asked at interviews, together with suggested answers. DO NOT attempt to commit the answers to memory. Think about how *you* would make your answers relevant to your own situation.

Some of the questions are **Competency Based** interview questions. They are designed to find out how you react to and behave in a given situation. They focus on a **specific** skill or skill set.

When faced with a competency based question you will be expected to give an example in order to demonstrate how proficient you are with a competency or skill. They are typically open-ended questions such as: *'Describe a situation when you were...'* or *'Tell me about a time when you...'* A frequently asked competency based question is: *'Describe a situation when you had to work to an important deadline'*.

These questions can appear at any point in an interview and it's important that your answer is **structured** and **clear**.

## 1. Tell me about yourself.

Probably the most common question asked in interviews.

You need to have a short statement prepared in your mind. Be careful that is doesn't come across as rehearsed. Focus on work-related items unless instructed otherwise. If you have little or no work experience the interviewer may want to know about your experience at school, college or university. Your experiences there may show early signs of leadership or that you are a strong team player.

Enjoying a personal challenge will earn you extra points. Talk about things you have done and other tasks accomplished that **relate** to the position you are interviewing for.

19

✓ Start with the item farthest back and work up to the present.

## 2. What do you know about our company?

This question is the one reason you need to do some research on the organisation before the interview. There is a wealth of information readily available. As recommended in *Chapter 1*, check the website, read the company brochure, press-cutting or newsletter.

✓ Find out how many employees they have, how many locations, divisions etc. Are they part of a larger group?

✓ Remember what was said about every industry having a trade paper or magazine. Buy or borrow a copy of a recent issue.

✓ While waiting to be invited into the interview check the coffee table or notice board for press cuttings or the company newsletter. Don't forget the earlier advice regarding the company's Annual Report and Accounts.

## 3. What experience do you have in this field?

Speak about the specifics that relate to the position you are applying for.

✓ Add **structure** to your response by following the STAR acronym. The letters stand for: SITUATION, TASK, ACTION, RESULT.

Interestingly, research among *Fortune 500* CEOs revealed a significant number of them were drawn towards candidates who demonstrated a **positive mental attitude**, to the point where, given a choice between two candidates of a similar background, the one with a positive mental attitude usually got the job. Furthermore, it was suggested that employing somebody who lacked experience but demonstrated the right attitude meant he or she was less likely to bring 'baggage' which might need to be 'unlearned'.

## 4. Do you consider yourself successful?

Why on earth would you say no? The answer **must** be 'yes', followed by a brief explanation. You must be able to demonstrate an ability to **set goals** and explain how you **achieved** them. Use the structured approach as suggested in Q3.

✗ Do not reveal confidential information even if asked to do so. This could be a trap to test your loyalty and discretion.

## 5. How would your work colleagues describe you?

Be prepared with a quote or two from your immediate manager or co-worker.

✓ Either a specific statement or paraphrase will work, eg. '*John O'Neill once introduced me as a rising star and on course to take over a new department. Shortly afterwards, I was promoted to position X.*'

## 6. Why did you leave your last job?

Stay **positive** regardless of the circumstances.

✗ Never refer to a problem with management and never criticise your previous employer or work colleagues. If you do, you'll be the one looking bad.

If you believe that you've gone as far as you can in your current job it's OK to say so and then explain that you're looking for a new challenge and new opportunity.

## 7. What have you done to improve your knowledge in the last year?

Try to include improvement activities that relate to your job. A wide variety of activities can be mentioned as **positive self-improvement**. Magazines or books you've read, for example. Training courses and seminars you've attended, and so on…

## 8. Are you applying for other jobs?

Be **honest** but don't spend too much time in this area. Keep the **focus** on this job and what you feel you can bring to the party by way of experience and added value.

## 9. Why do you want to work for this organisation?

If you've done your homework you should have a clear idea of why you'd like to join. If not, why are you there?

✓ Relate your ambitions to your long-term career goals.

If you've gone as far as you can with your present employer, say so. You could have worked for a family-owned business where family comes first and opportunities are limited.

## 10. Do you know anyone who works for us?

Be careful to only mention a friend if they are **respected.**

✓ Be aware that they may have a policy on close relatives working for the organisation.

## 11. What kind of salary are you looking for?

You might respond by referring to the **salary scale** in the advertisement and ask: '*How does it work?*' Or, you might say that you'd be looking to enter at the higher end of the pay scale and then remain quiet...the first one to speak is the loser.

Alternatively, you might feel more at ease giving details of your **current package** which would include basic salary, performance-related bonus and a company pension scheme.

## 12. Are you a team player?

This is a negative question. Why would anybody say 'no'?

✓ Be sure to have **examples** ready.

Specific examples that show how you've performed for the good of the team rather than for the good of yourself are relevant. Be careful not to brag or boast or sound superior.

## 13. How long would you expect to work for us if hired?

You should make it clear that you see this as a long-term commitment. If hired you would expect to be there for a number of years.

### 14. Have you ever had to fire anyone? How did you feel about it?

This is serious.

    ✗    Do not make light of it or come across as being hard and without feeling or sentiment.

You might say: '*I fully understand that there may be times when this is unavoidable. Hopefully it would be the last resort. If I was happy that all possible alternatives had been fully explored and that terminating the employment was the only option remaining, I would explain that to the person involved.*'

Add that you appreciate that firing is not the same as being made redundant or a need to downsize.

### 15. What is your philosophy toward work?

The interviewer is not looking for a long or flowery dissertation. '*Do you have strong feelings that the job gets done?*' '*Yes*'. That is the type of answer which works best here.

**Short** and **positive**. Choose words which demonstrate a **benefit** to the organisation. You may like to quote the immortal words of Winston Churchill when, in 1941, he addressed students at his old school. He famously left them with this one piece of advice:

'*Never, never, never give up.*'

Determination is an ingredient in the recipe for success.

### 16. What are your goals for the future? Or…Where do you see yourself in five years?

Your answer should **relate** to the position and the company you are interviewing with. Let it be known that one of your long-term goals is to be part of a company **intent on growth** and you'd like to be part of the process.

Add that you expect to **learn** and take on **additional responsibilities**. If relevant, say that you'd like to move into management.

### 17. Have you ever been asked to leave a position?

If you have not, say no.

If you have, be honest. Be brief and avoid saying negative things about the people or organisation involved.

### 18. Explain how you would be an asset to this organisation.

You should welcome this question as it gives you a chance to **highlight** your best points as they relate to the position being discussed.

✓ Before the interview write a list of your **strengths** and **areas for improvement**.

**Never** use the word **weakness**.

Re-stated, every weakness can be presented as an **area for improvement**. You should be able to say what is you bring that will have a positive impact.

### 19. Why should we hire you?

Point out how and why you sincerely believe that your strengths and experiences are a perfect **match** for the qualities the company listed in the advertisement.

✓ Say that what you've heard today reinforces that belief.

If you have a background in sales you should be able to express your qualities in terms of **features** and **benefits**.

### 20. Tell me about a time when you worked in a successful team and what made it successful.

The acronym TEAM...Together Everyone Achieves More is so true. Think of an occasion when you were part of a small group or team that achieved success. Ask yourself:

*'Was the project **approached** in any way that was different to previous projects?'*

*'Did the team **do** anything differently?'*

24

*'**What** was the role of the team leader or coach?'*

*'**Why** was that particular project so successful?'*

*'**How** did the team feel afterwards?'*

✓ Re-live the experience in your mind and, if it helps, follow your STAR approach. SITUATION, TASK, ACTION, RESULT.

## 21. What irritates you most about your co-workers?

This is a trap question.

✓ Think really hard but fail to come up with anything specific that irritates you.

If pressed, you might like to refer to punctuality at meetings – something everyone can understand and relate to.

## 22. What is your greatest strength?

You should have a few at your fingertips. Some examples are: an ability to **prioritise**, your **problem-solving** skills, your ability to **work under pressure**, your ability to **focus** on projects, your **professional expertise**, your **leadership** skills and your **communication** skills.

Be ready to expand on your answer with a specific example.

## 23. Do you have a weakness?

Everybody has a weakness. Begin by explaining how you've learned to replace the word 'weakness' with '**area for improvement**'.

**Note:** Practitioners of NLP (Neuro-Linguistic Programming) have shown that by substituting a negative word or phrase with a positive one the brain creates a pathway to search for a solution. So, instead of saying: '*giving presentations is a weakness*', say: '*giving presentations is an area for improvement*'.

Think of something that will not have a negative impact on the job.

✓ Choose something you are actively working on in an attempt to move it from an area for improvement to a **strength**.

### 24. Why do you think you would do well at this job?

You should be able to demonstrate a **track record**. The detail may be in your CV. Give several reasons, include skills and experience and try to relate your answer to the new role.

### 25. Tell me about your plans for *Continuing Personal Development.*

You should look at this question as having **two parts**. The two questions, rolled into one, are: '*What have you done in the past?*' and '*What plans do you have for the future?*'

The first part is similar to, but not the same as, Q7. You would be wise to have details of courses/classes attended, exams taken, certificates, diplomas etc. and relevant books and articles that you have read.

The word '*continuing*' is there to gauge your **attitude** towards **personal development**. Have you already signed up to an activity that will help you move forward in your career?

✓ Be aware: the interviewer is looking for signs or evidence of action taken for self-improvement.

### 26. What kind of person would you refuse to work with?

Refusing to work with someone should be a last resort.

✓ State that you would much prefer to seek to **engage** with the individual and make them part of the team. However, if he or she was openly disloyal to the organisation, violent or law-breaking, then you would not want to have them as a colleague.

### 27. What is more important to you: the money or the work?

Explain that, whilst money is important to you, there needs to be a **balance**.

We all know that money worries can have a devastating effect on our ability to do productive work. They *are* intrinsically linked but you should say that you're looking for a good balance between pay and performance.

## 28. What would your previous employer say is your strongest point?

Think back to your list of strengths. Loyalty, determination, enthusiasm, leadership, team player, ability to delegate, creativity and perhaps problem-solving.

You should have at least one of these skills or you are heading for the door!

## 29. Tell me about a problem you have had with a supervisor.

Another trap! This may be a test to see if you will bad mouth your boss. You could say: '*we didn't always agree but it never got in the way of working together*'.

## 30. What has disappointed you about a job?

✗ Do not get trivial or negative.

The company you worked for may have had to delay a project for reasons beyond their control such as a move in exchange rates or having to put a project on hold to deal with an IT issue.

✗ Do not be critical.

✗ Under no circumstances should you divulge confidential information. Loyalty is an attractive trait. Disloyalty is not.

## 31. Tell me about your ability to work under pressure.

You might say that you thrive under certain types of pressure. Give an example that **relates** to the particular position you have applied for, eg. Tight deadlines, sudden changes in customer requirements or adjustments in team contributions due to illness.

## 32. Who else have you applied to or have interviews with?

27

If, for example, you are hoping for a career in accountancy, it is reasonable to expect that you've applied to others. What you can say is that **their** company is your **first** choice.

It is OK to mention other companies by name. This will show consistency and that you have high standards.

## 33. What motivates you to do your best on the job?

Research carried out in America and the UK in the 90s revealed a dichotomy. Whilst the three most important motivators were *Recognition, Responsibility* and *Reward*, employers felt that **reward** was the prime motivator whereas employees put **recognition** at the top of their list. A simple pat on the back for a job well done was a huge motivator for the thousands of employees who took part in the survey.

A safe response would be to say that being **part of a team** that gets the job done on time and within budget motivates you the most. Then give an example.

## 34. What lessons have you learned from previous bosses?

✓ Say you've learned from each and every boss.

Do not describe negative lessons but, instead, **focus** on those lessons that offered a positive opportunity for **growth**.

## 35. How would you know you were successful in this job?

The interviewer is looking for signs that you **set goals** and **monitor performance**. This implies that you will always know if **progress** is being made and if **action** is needed to get back on course.

It's often said that you cannot improve something without first being able to measure it.

## 36. Would you be willing to relocate if the job required it?

✓ If you think this question is likely to arise you should discuss it with your family prior to the interview.

**Be honest.** If the answer is yes, say so.

28

**✱** **Under no circumstances say yes if you don't mean it.**

If you take the job and then announce you're unwilling to move, your career might suffer. You could cause yourself and your family a lot of grief – not to mention the interviewer.

## 37. What have you learned from your mistakes?

Try to turn a negative experience (a mistake) into a positive one, such as not giving up too soon.

✓ Admit to learning that the first solution is not always the best solution.

All too often the second solution produces a better result whereas going with the first solution to jump off the page **closes** the mind to other possibilities.

## 38. Give me an example of something you accomplished and something you were disappointed with.

The best way to respond is to give an example of something you accomplished that is **directly related** to the job you are interviewing for.

It is OK to check your CV for dates and events:

✓ Find the best match and explain how that experience will be beneficial to the position you are seeking.

The second part of the question can be dealt with by using an example of something that happened **outside of your control**.

## 39. What have you learned from mistakes on the job?

✓ Turn this negative question into something positive.

Give two examples! Start with a lesson you learned on a course such as the dangers of price cutting to get sales and then give an example of a well-intentioned mistake that you'll never forget – such as working ahead of colleagues on a project that delayed an outcome.

## 40. Do you have any *blind spots*?

This is a trick question. If you know about blind spots, they are no longer blind spots.

You might say that when you looked at the Annual Report and Accounts it was clear that you had a lot to learn as far as 'business finance' is concerned.

### 41. If you were hiring a person for this job, what would you look for?

It's unlikely that you will have seen the *job description* at this point but there may have been clues in the **advertisement**.

Try to introduce the same **key words** in your answer because research shows that **mirroring** language is known to build rapport and trust.

✓    Pick the qualities that they are looking for and relate them to your own qualities and experience.

### 42. How would you describe customer service?

The interviewer wants to know what you consider to be good and above average quality customer service. Try to give an example of what you would describe as excellent or outstanding customer service.

They may want to hear things like:

✓    'Good customer service means having a **thorough knowledge** of the product or service on offer.'

✓    'Good customer service is treating customers as you would like to be treated.'

✓    'Good customer service means helping customers by **asking questions**, **listening** and **matching their needs** with the appropriate benefits of the product or service on offer and to **never assume**.'

### 43. How do you propose to compensate for your lack of experience?

First, if you do have some experience, then share it and educate the interviewer.

Also, point out (if true) that you are conscientious, a hard worker and a quick learner.

## 44. What qualities do you look for in a boss?

✓ Be **generic** and **positive**.

Safe qualities are: leadership, knowledgeable, a sense of humour, fair and loyal to the team. All bosses believe they have these traits.

## 45. Tell me about a time when you helped resolve a dispute between others.

✓ Pick a specific incident.

✓ Concentrate on your problem-solving technique and not the dispute you settled.

✓ Focus on the **method** and not the content.

Be careful not to divulge personal or sensitive information.

## 46. What position do you prefer in a team working on a project?

A straightforward question calls for a straightforward answer.

If you are comfortable in different roles you will be seen as adaptable. It's good to point that out.

## 47. Who inspires you and why?

In 2009 a survey in the UK of over a thousand 13-19 year olds produced some interesting results:

 64% were inspired by someone in their family. Two in three (67%) believe there are more celebrities setting a bad example than a good one.

Today, however, it's probable that the late Steve Jobs of Apple would feature highly on a list of inspirational leaders, joining Bill Gates, Martin Luther King and Nelson Mandela.

Everybody is inspired by somebody,

31

✓ Think about who you'll put on the top of your list.

## 48. What has been your biggest professional disappointment?

✓ Be sure that you refer to something that was **beyond your control**.

✓ Show **acceptance** and no negative feelings.

## 49. Tell me about the most fun you have had on the job.

✓ For 'fun' read '**satisfaction**'.

You should be able to describe occasions when you enjoyed **success** and use this opportunity to show your **strengths** as a team member.

## 50. Do you have any questions for me?

✓ **Always** have some questions prepared.

The questions should show that you will be an asset to the organisation.

✓ Ask about the **job description** itself, **training** and **career development** but NOT about holidays, company perks or pay rises.

In *Chapter 1* I mentioned KPIs. This question gives you an excellent opportunity to ask if the company has **specific key performance indicators**.

It is sometimes the case that *all* of the questions you've prepared will have been covered. In this instance:

✓ Check your notes and hold up your list to show that you came prepared with questions but that you're satisfied that everything has been covered.

# TOP TIPS: FOR THE INTERVIEWER

Many candidates will be nervous. So too may you. Just as the interviewee needs to prepare for the interview, so must the person conducting it.

    ✓   Have a list of pre-prepared questions.

It is good to remember that you are also being evaluated and, in the eyes of the candidate, you *are* the company. Both parties are weighing each other up.

At the beginning, set the scene by explaining the **procedure** and do whatever you can to create a **relaxed atmosphere**. If the candidate remains nervous it could be down to you.

    ✓   Make a point of taking your mobile/cell phone out of your pocket or desk and switch it off.

    ✓   Switch of your computer/monitor.

In the next hour you could change someone's life forever and these gestures will speak louder than words.

## Author's own experience.

When you read about me at the end of this text you will probably discover two things:

1. I'm probably older than you.

2. I probably have more experience than you.

In all my 40 years of working in business, I have never had formal training in interviewing skills. Yet, against that background, I have interviewed a huge number of people – from the most junior to the most senior – and I have never admitted to my lack of training! After all, I was a manager and all managers know how to interview, don't they?

At this point I would like to publicly apologise to the many people I 'practised' on in my early years.

It was true then, and remains so today, that the moment a business card has the word *manager* added there is an assumption that that person is perfectly capable of conducting an interview. Right? Wrong. Looking back, I shudder to think of the mistakes I made. Perhaps you will learn from my mistakes:

- ✗ I did most of the talking.

- ✗ I relied heavily on gut reaction and instinct.

- ✗ I often made up my mind the moment the candidate walked into the room.

- ✗ If the candidate held my interest, I would extend the interview…and keep others waiting.

- ✗ At the time, I boasted of having an open door policy (I must have read that that was what successful managers did) and, if my secretary needed a document signed or had a customer on the phone, it was perfectly acceptable for her to interrupt us. In my ignorance I probably thought it would impress the candidate as he or she would see how important I was. It fed my ego. I thought it probably impressed my secretary too.

- ✗ There was no structure to the interview. 12 candidates. 12 different interviews.

- ✗ When the last candidate had left the building I would have trouble remembering who I had seen.

34

Hopefully, this book will have helped you to learn from my mistakes and avoid suffering from 'candidate confusion'.

It really is not that difficult to find a **system** that will work for you. If you are unable to recall details of all the interviewees you could end up hiring the wrong candidate – why not ask permission to take a **photograph** and avoid an expensive mistake?

✓ Treat each candidate as you would like to be treated if the positions were reversed.

✓ Review the list of questions you plan to ask and avoid the trap of asking a string of negative questions at the beginning. Candidates will, inevitably, be nervous so help them to relax by getting off to a **positive start** with positive questions.

Apart from policemen, members of the armed forces and insurance assessors, it's my experience that professionally trained interviewers are few and far between.

✓ Check out current legislation on **equality in the workplace**. Interviewers need to ensure that every candidate gets asked the same questions, particularly at the beginning. Follow up questions may be influenced by the answers right up to the last question asked.

# TOP TIPS: DO'S AND DON'TS

## Before you walk into the interview room:

✓ Do remind yourself of how good you are.

✓ Do review your list of strengths.

✓ Do think about past successes.

✓ Do remind yourself that you've already achieved your first goal: you and your CV got you here.

✓ Do check that your phone is switched off or on 'silent'.

✓ Do be aware that on the other side of the door, someone has just read, or is reading, your CV.

✓ Do make sure you are able to recall key points and dates on your CV.

✓ Do check for spelling mistakes – or get someone else to do it for you.

✓ Do check that you have everything you need with you.

✓ Do have a final look in the mirror and **smile**.

✓ Do stand tall and walk in with an air of confidence.

You are ready. Good luck.

## But remember...

✗ Don't underestimate the value of preparation.

✗ Don't do a PowerPoint presentation that contains spelling or grammar mistakes.

- ✗ Don't allow negative thoughts to enter your mind.

- ✗ Don't smoke before the interview – the smell can be very objectionable to some people.

- ✗ Don't carry your coffee into the room with you. Chances are you'll spill it on the new carpet.

- ✗ Don't answer a text message in the middle of the interview.

- ✗ Don't explain to the interviewer where their organisation is going wrong and how you will put it all right.

- ✗ Don't arrive late.

- ✗ Don't argue!

Thank you for reading **Top Tips: Interviews**. I hope that you have found it a valuable resource.

# OTHER **TOP TIPS** TITLES

*Top Tips:* Writing a CV/Résumé

*Top Tips:* Selling

*Top Tips:* Negotiating

*Top Tips:* Goal Setting

*Top Tips:* Communication

*Top Tips:* Time Management

*Top Tips:* Creative Thinking

*Top Tips:* Problem Solving

*Top Tips:* Effective Delegation

# About The Author

John Hodgson is widely known as a successful businessman and business consultant.

He has 20 years of experience working with *Philips Consumer Products* in the UK and Overseas.

He was Managing Director of *Mandev Training*, *Gooding International* and a board member of *Race Electronics*.

He was a founder of *RH International* and *OEM Services* with offices in the USA, Hong Kong, Taiwan and a joint venture in Xiamen, China.

John is a senior lecturer at the *Institute of Directors* and works with hundreds of individuals representing a diverse group of blue chip organisations.

Author of *Test Your Financial Awareness* published by Hodder & Stoughton and ***Top Tips:*** *Writing a CV/Résumé*.

# ACKNOWLEDGEMENTS

My grateful thanks must go to the following people, without whom this book might never have been written. Their wisdom, support and advice is much appreciated:

Charlotte Choules

Annie Clarke

Frank Clarke

Kevin Hempson

Christina Hughes

Dr Lynn Morgan

Dr Samantha Rayner

Terry Riley

Graeme Udall

Jack Sutcliffe

# WITH SPECIAL THANKS TO

 Anglia Ruskin
University

Charlotte Choules is studying the post-graduate MA Publishing course at Anglia Ruskin University, Cambridge, 2011/2012.

She has shown real initiative and enthusiasm for her career in publishing by volunteering to help with the design, formatting, editing and proof-reading of this book and the *Top Tips* series.

The end result is testament to the course and tutors.  My thanks also to Anglia Ruskin University for allowing and, indeed, encouraging her participation.

For information on the course go to:
www.anglia.ac.uk/ruskin/en/home.html

## Notes

Notes

# Notes

.